# TREASURES
## FROM DARK PLACES

Inspirations from the
Reservoirs of God's love

# THARAN GARDINER BRICE

WESTBOW
PRESS®
A DIVISION OF THOMAS NELSON
& ZONDERVAN

WestBow Press books may be ordered through booksellers or by contacting:

WestBow Press
A Division of Thomas Nelson & Zondervan
1663 Liberty Drive
Bloomington, IN 47403
www.westbowpress.com
1 (866) 928-1240

ISBN: 978-1-5127-8260-8 (sc)
ISBN: 978-1-5127-8261-5 (e)

Library of Congress Control Number: 2017905413

Print information available on the last page.

WestBow Press rev. date: 12/28/2017

# INTRODUCTION~ PREFACE

Now it's time to reveal to the world what The Lord has been building in me ~Purpose!!!!!!

The pain that comes from brokenness is oftentimes the point of conception for the many gifts that lie dormant within us. It is at some of the most tumultuous times in life that we experience a type of labour giving birth *to* many talents and skills which were made readily available as they matured in the incubator known as life's obstacles. The apostle Paul puts it like this in Romans 8:18 KJV~" *"For I reckon that the sufferings of this present time are not worthy to be compared with the glory which shall be revealed in us."* It was in the times of pain that I delivered giving birth to the "treasures "that were housed in this earthen vessel. Process is painful but profitable!

There is nothing more invigorating than exerting energy into that which we are most passionate about!

## *Meditation:*

I am so grateful that I matter enough to Him that He meets me wherever I am regardless of what I'm doing. He affirms, counsels, chastises, revives, refreshes, restores and ministers to me not just when it's convenient for Him but whenever it is needed.

*"For He knows our frame; He remembers that we are dust." ~ Psalms 103:14NKJV*

# TREASURES IN THE DEEP

Some people are comfortable on the shore line so long as they can find a means of existence there. I am not of this persuasion. I belong in the deep places where the treasures are. There's the risk of becoming overwhelmed in the pursuit of the deep, but the success that lies ahead is worth it. I believe that fear and its crippling effects keep many from the pursuit of such greatness that lies there but I refuse to be dominated, restrained or anchored by fear. I want what's mine! It's there for the taking!

On the shore line I can only have what comes to me. When I BOLDLY launch into the deep, I can have all that awaits me in the storehouse and so much more. Courage, determination and faith drives me there!

# MY LIFE

*I was brought up in a family where there was always a practiced form of godliness, but as I grew older I came to the realization that the personal relationship with God was a very shallow one. Ursula, my older cousin was the only one that I knew who professed Christianity. At the age of twelve with a limited knowledge of Christianity, I knew that a Christian was who I wanted to be. My life is a testimony of the grace, mercy and faithfulness of God.*

*On August 30th, 1973 the lives of Delvera Richardson and Wellington Gardiner changed as they became the parents of a six pound baby girl whom they named Tharan Anneth Gardiner. I hold in the hallways of my heart many fond childhood memories. Being taught by my grandmother, Martha Lenore Saunders to recite two very familiar prayers stand out like the breaking of day amidst them all. I later learnt that these simple prayers were the foundation of a lifestyle of prayer and a faith that would allow me to maneuver through the many storms of life. My Sundays consisted of a dinner that included peas and rice, fried chicken, potato salad and macaroni. Church attendance and listening to songs by the Cooling Waters gospel group was the order of the day. As I reflect it seemed as though Sunday was the highlight of the week, every other day seemed insignificant. In a special reservoir of memories are cherished thoughts of my relationship with my father which were times of laughter, love and tears. My mother taught me to always go after the best. Even when my decisions caused her pain she remained faithful in supporting me as best as she knew how.*

*Being the eldest of five siblings made me acquainted with many aspects of motherhood. I've experienced eleven years of academic excellence but the twelfth year was a struggle due to teenage pregnancy. I believe it all started when my mother left to find her long lost father who* had made his way to Abaco under a secret identity. I can recall many days wishing that she was with us.

She continued to support us and we often visited but I wanted her here where we were. Amidst the emotional struggles I became actively involved as an Acolyte, a chorister and the Vice President of the Christian Youth Movement of a local Anglican Church. She cheered me on from where she was! Despite my involvement in these activities there was still a void that I was unable to fill. This was the initiation of a quest for love which landed me in some relationships where I had loved more than I was loved. I gave birth to five children that were fathered by four men. I had become an acquaintance of disappointment, rejection, hurt and financial duress which were the results of single parenting.

With a tenacious determination to break free from the grip of the generational curses that has held many of my relatives captive I found refuge and fortitude in my faith in God. On February 28th 2004 I was joined in holy matrimony to Dwight Engleburt Brice, the biological father of my youngest child and the man who courageously adopted the four elder children, hence my name was changed to Tharan Anneth Brice. By that union I was officially the mother of a sixth child, my husband's oldest biological son. I have spent the majority of my employment years in the area of customer service which afforded me a wealth of experience in the 'how to' and 'how not to' of this area. Being faced with oppression and suppression on the job has propelled me into the decision to pursue a Bachelor of Arts degree in Human Resource Management. That degree I never attained, however, I managed to get a certification in Human Resources. My greatest motivation in this pursuit was to make a significant difference in the way that people were treated on the job.

Past problems and pains have afforded me the privilege of giving birth to many gifts, talents and hobbies which include prayer, makeup application, inspirational writing, motivational speaking, a tenacious desire for ministry and a keen eye for fashion. Every one of my life's experiences whether good or bad has worked out for my good and God's glory. Today, because of the furnace of affliction I am a mentor to many, a youth leader, an intercessor an author and a life coach. My philosophy in life is "There is a way to do it better, find it!" (Abraham Lincoln)

## *Meditation:*

*Zechariah 4:7King James Version (KJV)*
*7 Who art thou, O great mountain? before Zerubbabel thou shalt become a plain: and he shall bring forth the headstone thereof with shoutings, crying, Grace, grace unto it.*

# THE INSERT ~ A CLIP FROM OUR SON'S OBITUARY

When I began putting this manuscript together all six of my children were alive. On the 18th of July 2015 that has changed our son DiMaggio has since went on to be with the Lord. My life has shifted from waiting to that of take action now! Understanding that "Now" is the accepted time. This page I chose to dedicate to him and the legacy he's left behind. Do all you can while you can.

*Ecclesiastes 9:10King James Version (KJV)*
*10 Whatsoever thy hand findeth to do, do it with thy might; for there is no work, nor device, nor knowledge, nor wisdom, in the grave, whither thou goest.*

It is my persuasion that this pain will give birth to revival, salvation and restoration! You have taught me to love in the midst of difficulties. Never one day have you ever disrespected me not even in the smallest way. I was convinced that you'd be one of the preachers from our clan (that you were). Preacher, evangelist comedian soloist and a debonair, Dimaggio was all of these. I vowed to love you and to cover you in prayer. Mission accomplished, that I did. Thank you Father for loaning me an angel, thank you Michelle for trusting me to be his other mom, thank you Dwight for believing that I was capable and qualified to love him unconditionally . Yes, I call you my son. Rest in peace; one day you will Rise in power. Shalom.

Your other mom- Tharan Brice

IT IS IN PAIN THAT WE GIVE BIRTH TO THAT WHICH IS PRICELESS.

For so long I had believed the lies that Satan has told. I was dressed up, made up, smelling sweet, smiling but messed up and broken. I was told by people and circumstances that I wasn't good enough. I wasn't good enough for the son, I wasn't good enough for the loan, I wasn't good enough for marriage, ministry or a promotion. They thought that I wasn't good enough for the clothes that I wore or the furniture that I owned.

God was constantly saying "YOU ARE ENOUGH!" I'd say that I believed Him but then I'd still hold on to Satan's lies. Everything that didn't work out whispered "you're not good enough."

BUT GOD..........

One of the greatest battles we will ever fight is the one that is internal. The internal wars are the ones we fight against ourselves. They are the ones that rage from within.

# THE SHIFT

*We have spent so many years polluting ourselves with negativity, which when collaborated transfers into sickness and diseases which manifest within the body, mind, soul or spirit contaminating the very essence of who we are short-circuiting our lifespan, consequently depriving us of what God has pre-ordained as our best life. In order to survive we must now retrain ourselves and unlearn the thoughts, ideas and opinions that we have carried about as truth. We must now find a way to unlearn and purge ourselves of years of toxins that we have collected by way of relationships, life's experiences, poor choices and corrupted connections. This may mean walking away from the comfort zone and disconnecting from everything that was once relied on as a means of support. Sometimes we must lose in order that we may win.*

*One day I opted to walk away from a life that was thought to have sustained my family and me for years. It was a move that most persons considered uncalculated and of no financial sense. However, I am convinced it was a move that will positively shift the spiritual, physical and financial temperature of not only my life but additionally the lives of those that God has divinely connected me to. I chose to go with my gift. It has and will make room for me!*

*Proverbs 18:16 King James Version (KJV)*
*[16] A man's gift maketh room for him, and bringeth him before great men.*

# A GOD GIVEN DREAM

A God given dream tends to make you and those around you uncomfortable. Perhaps it's because they have some sort of idea of the challenges and boundaries that life has presented you with. A God given dream is greater than your financial resources and oftentimes supersedes ones educational, vocational, geographical, sociological or biological background. They cause our seams to burst! They stir up both internal and external storms because to accomplish them requires far more than our human abilities but additionally faith and confidence in our supernatural God.

I used to desire to be validated by loved ones and friends. That's all changed! I once bought a dress that few found attractive. The dress turned heads and of course it induced questions and comments. Whoa!!!!! The silent stares screamed "what possessed you to buy and even so wear that dress?"

It was plaid and the style of it required lots of fabric. To me it was beautiful. My husband's facial expression was a compelling one. It gripped my self-esteem and demanded that I place the dress to the deepest part of the closet never to be seen again! In that moment something extraordinary happened. I kept pressing the dress and with that bold action I was blessed with a spiritual revelation. What I carry is unique, uncommon and grand! It's beyond average or ordinary. Many will not and cannot comprehend it. It has been placed in me by the All Powerful God. The Great I Am! I've often looked for those equal to me to validate me when they really couldn't. My validation must come from the one who created me and impregnated me with that which I carry. He alone possesses the capacity to fully comprehend the depth, width, breadth, length and height of the holy seed that I have been called, chosen and predestined to carry. It is a great mission and assignment to make an indelible mark in time and eternity. He alone being God the creator, the sovereign one possess the power and authority to validate a gift of this magnitude.

# MY QUESTION REVEALED HIS ANSWER

## My question

"God, what is it that hinders my complete trust in you? I realize that for years the core of every word or message you've ever given me involved both TRUST and SURRENDER."

## His Answer

"Disappointment has delayed your ability to completely trust. The enemy has used delay, denial, disappointment and rejection to retard your ability to wholly trust."

Absolutely nothing in this universe happens without a knock on the door called permission or access from Our Creator. He is both strategic and intentional. Whenever he permits IT whatever that it may represent, his intent is for a showdown and the end result of destroying the enemy and making a show of him openly. Ask Pharaoh whose heart was hardened resulting in the showdown at The Red Sea, a testimony that spoke to ages past and speaks to the present and those that are yet to come. God knows not only the beginning and the end; his spirit transcends the journey in between.

## Confession and prayer

Father, I realize that the many no's, disappointments, rejections, apparent failures, loss, defeat and denial have held me captive for many years constraining my complete yes. I acknowledge you from within the belly of this great fish recognizing that you alone possess the ability to speak to this great fish commanding it to spit me up along with every message that you have placed within me. Heaven, hell and the earth must give way to your will for my life.

Empower me Oh Lord, my Adonai to receive from you by way of a submissive spirit that wholly surrenders with a complete yes. Let my mind, my heart, my soul and spirit harmonize a synchronised "yes Lord" in complete surrender. Let the gates of iron and brass be broken down and every ceiling be shattered that the investments that you have made in me may herald a message of deliverance to mankind.

*"Long my imprisoned spirit lay, fast bound in sin and natures night, thine eye diffused a quickening ray, I woke, the dungeon flamed with light.*

*My chains fell off, my heart was free, I rose, went forth and followed Thee!" (Charles Wesley, 1707-1788)*

# BEAUTIFUL GARMENTS

For years I got naked with people who couldn't bear to see my scars and again I'd experience a type of rejection. When I sought love and believed to have found her, I'd get comfortable enough to remove my beautiful garments. I was convinced that I could un-robe revealing the scars that my true love had carefully covered. Once the scars were revealed they couldn't bear the sight; some scorned, some scoffed, some walked away whilst others hid themselves. Again my true love would wash me in the perfume of his word and robe me again in my beautiful garments. It took years and many relationships for me to learn that I couldn't be intimate with everyone that I loved.

*To appoint unto them that mourn in Zion, to give unto them beauty for ashes, the oil of joy for mourning, the garment of praise for the spirit of heaviness; that they might be called trees of righteousness, the planting of the LORD, that he might be glorified. Isaiah 61:3 KJV*

# LET US PRAY!!!

Father set us free from the prison walls that the enemy has fortified with anger, hurt, disappointment, rejection and frustration. Break us out through your anointing that this very same anointing would be effectually at work in us and through us. Father set us free that we may be effective witnesses! Set us free that our witness will be with credence! Shut off the gates of our lives to satanic poachers and destiny altering demonic forces! Shatter ever brazen altar we have knowingly and unknowingly erected! Dismantle the pillows of unbelief, fear, stubbornness, pride and rebelliousness! Instead erect the altar of righteousness that we may walk worthy of the vocation to which we have been called living soberly and righteously! Lay your battle axe to the root of every evil tree that was planted in our lives destroying its branches leaves fruits and seeds that they have produced! Release your fire to consume its remains in Jesus' name! Gird our loins with truth father that we may be changed and positively affect change! Teach us to respond spiritually according to the directives of your word which is quick powerful and sharp rather than carnally according to the works of our flesh! Father quicken us to mortify the deeds of our flesh that we may not reap the corruption thereof! Father, hedge in our families and our marriages for we know that when the hedge is removed the serpent will bite! Send angelic assistance and reinforcement to guard our borders for you are The Lord of Sabaoth! Assign warring Angels to help us to war against the host of hell even as our Intercessor and advocate intercedes on our behalf according to your will Father! Release your people oh God from the enemy's yokes and burdens! We cancel the spirit of suicide, hopelessness, contention and discord in Jesus' name! We declare and decree that your banner over us is love, peace, unity, joy, healing and wholeness! Father, cause us to have all things in common and be on one accord that you may fill us with your Holy Spirit and endow us with power and the anointing that we may do the greater works setting captives free through the unction of this power vested in us!

# EMANCIPATION

Every scar and every issue that I've ever been faced with has a God ordained purpose. That purpose is no longer to be tucked away in my personal archives; it all belongs to The Lord and to His people for His glory. The hurt, rejection, pain and disappointments were all ordained by God to make such a colourful message. Every season of my life produced a message and now this is the beginning of a new season and a new day. It is the time of divine release. Nothing will be wasted .What I once thought were the lemons of life were really the most vital ingredient to make a refreshing drink of lemon aid not only for me but for those to whom He has assigned me. The so called mess produced a message, the disappointments housed my appointments, and the rejections were the affirmation of God's calling on my life. The series of brokenness was God's way of validating me.

# FOREWORD ~ NOTES FROM MY FRIENDS

*Hey lady,*

*You are a bold yet humble, nonjudgmental, intelligent, outgoing, outspoken, admirable, encouraging, praying, inspirational woman of God, wife, mother, grandmother, daughter, granddaughter, niece, aunt, sister, friend, acquaintance. You are always willing to listen, share, offer advice, take advice, and stand by those you love and trust. You are willing to help whenever necessary, give your last, take on the burden of others, conquer and divide, squash the enemy and find time for God on a daily basis.*

*Your friend,*
*Tanya Miller.*

# The Lady I know by Gaynell Robinson

*A woman of virtue, and strength, one who encourages & motivates*
*She has a passion for children and young people alike*
*An anointed woman of God, a mentor who's*
*Her hands are blessed by God through creativity*
*Though small in stature she possesses a great big heart*
*A prayer worrier, an intercessor*
*A wife, a mother, a confident and a true friend*
*I Love this Woman*
*Always willing to share and help*
*A servant's heart, will go beyond the call*
*An entrepreneur*
*She is my friend! ~ **Tharan Anneth Gardiner Brice***

*Tharan, my dear:*

*I do apologize for keeping you waiting so long. I never forgot. I just could not get my thoughts together. You are a sweetheart.*

*Terri.*

*"She is one of the most refreshing and pleasant persons I have ever known, and it is evident that she knows and meets with God on a daily basis.*

*I am confident that reading this book will be an enjoyable and fulfilling experience."*

Terri M. Antonio-Rolle
Executive Administrative Assistant to

Mr. Jerome E. Elliott, PE - AGM, Engineering
Bahamas Electricity Corporation
P. O. Box N-7509
Blue Hill & Tucker Roads
Nassau, THE BAHAMAS

# A NOTE FROM THE RESERVOIRS OF MY HEART. ~

After much hurt, brokenness, distress, rejection, disappointment and weeping over what it appeared I had lost I came to the conclusion through the aiding of the Holy Spirit that I'd rather risk losing their love for guiding them in the way that is righteous than gaining their love, honour and respect for turning a blind eye and remaining silent to that which is wrong.

I love my children deeper than any situation or circumstance that they can or ever will find themselves in. I hold the faith that their lives are in His hand and their actions are the epistle of their testimony.

To you my children I love you today, tomorrow and forever! You are one of the reasons I choose to STAND.

*"Therefore, since we are surrounded by such a great cloud of witness, let us throw off everything that hinders us and the sin that so easily entangles. And let us run with perseverance the race marked out for us." Heb. 12:1 NIV*

# THE INSCRIPTION

The inscription on these pages will bring its readers face to face with truth of some kind. I believe through divine revelation we will see ourselves under the microscope of this truth, thus unveiling the carnality of the flesh. It will bring rebuke, restoration, conviction and correction. You will discover every secret agenda of the enemy that may have been masked as human frailty and paraded as that which is acceptable.

# THE SHEDDING...

I experienced a shedding; the shedding of myself, the works of the flesh, carnality, pride, rebelliousness, selfishness and weight. When my faith was broken I cried and heaven cried with me and those tears brought forth DELIVERENCE.

From the pages of this book will flow life, hope, Instruction, inspirations and tranquillity.

# ACKNOWLEDGEMENT

Thank you Heavenly Father for using me. As you speak I will write for it is with your eyes you allow me to see, with your ears you allow me to hear and with your Spirit you reveal to my understanding. With my hand Lord you write and address mankind. Thank you to family, friends, teachers, mentors, spiritual leaders and my enemies you have all played a significant role.

**Confidence~ note from the author**

**May the Lord grant you the wisdom to recognize the open doors he has set before you and the courage to walk therein with an unwavering faith and confidence in Him.**

*"I know your works (Behold, I have set before you an open door, which no one can shut)….." (Revelation 3:8 Darby Bible Translation)*

# SHUT UP IN MY BONES!

There is a longing on the inside of us to have the love and support of those that we hold near and dear. At times we reflect on our personal accomplishments for whatever reason and feel a sense of inadequacy. It is at times such as these that the listening ear of a loved one makes the world of difference. The power of touching and agreeing has the ability to gather us up from the place of discouragement. Sometimes we just need to know that we are indeed making a significant difference, sometimes we need just to be held, cuddled and nourished at the breast of love. Sometimes we just need someone else to stand in our support rallying behind us letting us know that indeed "we can!"

Self-validation is important but I believe that it is the will of God that who and what we are and all that He intends for us to be is to be nurtured in the cradle of a loving family and friends who will help us to draw strength from the oasis of The Agape, Eros and Phileo love streams. These streams possess the God given ability to cause life to exist in the driest places. They will cause life, healing, deliverance and prosperity to come forth.

In times when we are starved of our physical support system the power of God has a way of quickening us as we pour out of our reserve into the lives of His people who may be in parched places. There is an anointing that flows when we step out of our emotions breaking its power to hinder our God given assignment. This same anointing propels us into the deepest reservoirs of the grace, favour and abundant supply of heaven's store house which flows from the Saviour's inexhaustible supply.

# EXPERIENCE, MY TEACHER

**Experience has been a great teacher but she teaches hard lessons.**

# NOOSED TO BE LOOSED ~
# A WOMAN'S PROSPECTIVE

Sometimes as women we are ridden by our emotions. We are noosed by life's circumstances. The vicissitudes of life is what it's called. Brokenness, rejection, disappointment, oppression, depression, suppression and all the other devices that the enemy uses to hold us captive so that we become marred with ashes diminishing the beauty of our souls and belittling our self-worth. The main objective is to weary us so that we find ourselves despondent and opting to neglect our call to greatness and divine alignment with the plans and purpose of God, purporting the feeling of unworthiness despite the anointing that works in and through us by the power of The Almighty, all powerful, all sufficient God.

# MY PATH

There is a path that my feet alone have been ordained to walk. No other but the Saviour can travel with me. Others will only know of the experiences through the words that I have been ordained to write. Along that path I encountered loneliness, despair, assassination, vexation, turmoil, weariness and brokenness.

I felt the cold callous grip of captivity. Out of this encounter is expected the harvest of praise, worship, thanksgiving, the anointing, deliverance and warfare. I endure the scorpion's sting, the snake's venomous bites, the flames of the fire, the waters of the flood and I am expected to endure not bearing the countenance of discomfort but instead the beauty of grace and godliness and singing the songs of Zion.

"I am taking you from a place of complaint to the place of endurance and contentment" says God. The race is not to the swift, neither the battle to the strong but to He who endures....

When we talk with God we should experience rest in the midst of the challenges that we face.

Some of us are not afforded the apparent luxury of complaining.

# LORD RENEW MY MIND

What we need is a regenerated mind! Unless our minds are renewed we are unable to accept the spiritual truths that are **written**. If we are unable to accept the written truth which is the word of God we cannot and will not be changed nor will our situations change. When we embrace the power of a transformed mind then we become empowered to bring about changes in systems!

Let it be known that it is the plan of the enemy to keep us distracted and drunk with the cares of this life. It is a strategy to keep our minds in turmoil making it difficult and often times impossible to hear God's voice and receive His directives. A chaotic mind is the enemy's warfare! It is in the Shalom of Abba that we find the answers to many circumstances and issues. It is in the Shalom that that which is hidden becomes exposed. If we allow our minds to dwell and be guarded by the Shalom of Abba we will receive the instructions needed to manoeuvre the vicissitudes of life.

**Do not conform to the pattern of this world, but be transformed by the renewing of your mind. Then you will be able to test and approve what God's will is...His good, pleasing and perfect will. (Romans 12:2 NIV)**

# PRAYER FOR THE MIND

Father, today in the name of Jesus Christ, I hijack every negative thought pattern. I bring my thoughts, ideas and opinions under Holy Ghost arrest in Jesus' name. I subdue and modify my thought pattern to reflect the mind of Christ .Father in the name of Jesus I root up, pluck up and dismantle the root of every ungodly, unruly, unproductive thought. I plead the blood of Jesus upon every word that was spoken by the directives of any demonic force to frustrate me and cause me to become dysfunctional in carrying out my God given purpose. In the name of Jesus the Christ, the Sacrificial Lamb of God I break down every satanic altar that has been set up against my mind-set to steal my peace and joy causing a disruption in my ability to think on the things that are good, honest, just, pure, lovely and praise worthy! Redeem my thoughts heavenly Father through the blood of Jesus and the anointing. I command every unruly thought to submit to the power of the name of Jesus Christ through the burden removing yoke destroying anointing of the Almighty God. I command the Holy Spirit to set up stakes with the blood of Jesus Christ around the perimeters of my mind that ward off any satanic intruder in the name of Jesus! Father in the name of Jesus Christ my Saviour and deliverer let my mind be in a constant renewal process with your word and right thinking. Father in the name of Jesus I cancel every word spoken into the atmosphere against my life that was contrary to your will and agenda for my life! Holy Spirit send your consuming fire to penetrate the arenas of my mind destroying anything and everything that does not reflect your order, directives and will for my life in Jesus' name. I loose my mind from every satanic attack in Jesus' name and I bind it to the word of God, to joy, to peace, to wisdom to creativity to purity, good health and wholeness in Jesus' name! Father you gave me the authority to bind and loose based on your word and the assurance that whatever I bind on earth is bound in heaven and whatever I loose on earth is loosed in heaven. Father in the name of Jesus download your wisdom that is from above to my mind and heart that I may forever be guided by you in all things and of sound judgement.

# SILENCE

In today's world silence seem to be primordial; yet I believe that sessional visits to the solitude of silence rewards an individual benefits that are nascent. Clarity, direction, instruction, intuition and revelation emerges from silence, however, many persons elude the halls of silence. To some persons silence is a closet in which gloom, doom and the horridness of some not so pleasant memories hangs. When we retreat to the solitude we stand face to face with our God and ourselves.

# THE RACE

Some people choose their careers out of desperation, others choose out of purpose. The difference between the two is that often times when we choose out of desperation it's just about the salary and benefits that may be attached. Choosing a career that is born out of purpose is one that brings to mind a runner in a close race. As the competitors approach the finish line which is the defining moment, one may be required to dip in order that the winner may be determined.

The athlete leans forward and projects the neck outward in order that he may be declared the victor. To the one looking on the position assumed by the runner may seem awkward, however, being the one in the race he fully understands his reasoning behind his actions despite the thoughts, opinions or lack of understanding expressed or experienced by onlookers. One might imagine that apart from looking strange the posture taken by the runner most likely presents some level of discomfort to him or her because he or she may be manoeuvring in an unnatural position.

Sometimes in life we are led to make decisions that are questionable by those around us and that may even make us experience the feeling of awkwardness but it's at those times when we are required to stick out our neck in order to seal or establish our defining moment. I believe that today I stand at the threshold of my defining moment. It is a lonely and an awkward place and exclusive to me. It's a place of many questions and uncertainties but unlimited possibilities. Though others would be affected by it ultimately I am the one with the exclusive rights. That right however makes it no less easy.

Today I acknowledge that where God needs us is much more important than where we want to be.

# THE CANDLE

In the absence of what we know as light we must rely on the small fire from a candle and or what we know about our environment. I wrestled with a decision and realized that I wrestled with the spirit of fear. I was instructed to turn on the light and look at myself in the mirror. The Spirit of the Lord sent me to the kitchen for a candle and a box of matches. I returned to my bedroom, turned off the light and made several failed attempts to light the candle. Finally, the flame embraced the wick. The Lord then instructed me to stand in the mirror holding the candle. What I saw was a huge shadow of myself. I asked the Lord for revelation and this is what came:

"Turn on the Light. "This I did. "Do you see the shadow?" He asked. My response was no. He then asked "does it mean it's not there?" I turned the light back off and continued staring at my shadow. Its size was amazing! Then I heard the words "in the absence of the familiar we are so much greater!" That shadow was a representation of all that God has placed in us, the unseen. *(Now faith is the substance of things hoped for, the evidence of things not seen. ~ Hebrews 11:1 KJV)*

The bible refers to the spirit of man as the candle of the Lord. (SEE Proverbs 20:27). The reality is a candle is most effective in darkness but the presence of other forms of light may appear to diminish the candle's light but in no way does the Candle really lose its potential. In this instance purpose and potential make themselves known. Purpose is what something is made to do whilst potential is all that it's capable of doing.

Sometimes we are required to function solely on what we know of God despite the external influences. Many of us at one point or another were afraid of our shadow but that's only because we failed to understand it. Our shadow is just a reminder of the greatness of God in us. It's the untapped potential that lies within us waiting to come out. Darkness which sometimes appears as uncertainties is one of the ways God may choose to reveal it. This was written in a dark room lit only by a candle.

There is so much more in you than what the light of your surroundings reveal but it's seen in the presence of a candle in the midst of darkness. I've noticed in the absence of the candle man's shadow appears regular.

I've seen beautiful plants grow from within rocks~ "ah the beauty of obscurity!"

# FATHER FORGIVE US

Father in the name of Jesus I acknowledge you. You are the author and finisher of our faith, the lifter up of our head, the custodian of our souls, the forgiver of our sins, and the healer of every disease.

Father, there is none like you! You are our righteousness, our High Priest who is touched with the feelings of our infirmities. You are our shelter, our hiding place, our bridge over troubled waters, our rock in a weary land, our way, the truth and our light that guides us.

Father today I thank you for the revelation of truth. Father please forgive us for we have failed in our kingdom assignments and sinned against you. Your word declares *"If my people, which are called by my name, shall humble themselves, and pray, and seek my face, and turn from their wicked ways; then will I hear from heaven, and will forgive their sin, and will heal their land."(2 Chronicles 7:14KJV)*

Father we have perfected our talk put failed miserably in our walk .When we should have loved we were angry, when we should have forgiven we were resentful, when we should have submitted we rebelled, when we should of prayed we condemned,when we should have pursued peace we fought, when we should have fought we stood still, when we should have helped to bring about healing we added injury, when we should have been praying we were having discussions, when we should have sought You our creator we sought the creation and when we should have been witnessing we were boasting in self-righteousness. Father, forgive us! When we should have been dressing and keeping the gardens that you have placed us in we allowed the serpent to beguile and distract us causing us to lose sight of our true assignment. We complained when we should have given thanks, we spoke curses when we should have spoken blessings and blessed what we should have cursed. We loved what we should have hated and hated that which we should have loved. We spoke out of turn and said nothing when it was our turn. When we should have rebuked in love we cloaked and caused destruction. Father we repent.

Thank you for showing us the error of our ways, not that we may condemn ourselves but that we may experience the godly sorrow that leads to repentance. Help us to remember that you chastise those you love, and punish each one you accept as your child.

Amen! SELAH ~Think and act on these things!

## UNDERSTANDING FAITH

Sometimes you've got to move on what you hear, understanding that faith cometh by hearing and hearing by the word. The bible says that faith is the substance of things hoped for and the evidence of the unseen thing. The just lives by what is known as this unseen faith. Anything that's alive shows signs of progression. Any great action or impact begins with a seed of thought. It is born out of something, that something is opportunity. Opportunity doesn't always manifest itself as just that. It shows itself disguised in crises, lack, failure, defeat, disappointment, dead ends or even oppression. An individual loaded with unusual potential may for a brief moment be fooled by the masquerade but soon leaps by faith and embraces the opportunity that lies ahead with great anticipation and expectancy. Greatness lies on the other side of this mountain. The mountain is just to show you what's in you .Everyone else need little or no convincing.

# CRISES~ THE OPPORTUNITY TO CREATE

Sometimes crises create the opportunity for a much needed change or challenge us to embrace creativity. Do something you've never done but always dreamt of doing. I am persuaded that if God permits a problem He is God enough to provide the solution.

**GOD'S PLANS FOR ME** ~ *"For I know the plans I have for you,"* *declares the Lord, "plans to prosper you and not to harm you, plans to give you hope and a future" (Jeremiah 29:11NIV)*

Dear Heavenly Father, thank you for the plans that you think towards me, plans of good and not of evil to give me hope and an expected end. Oh Lord, enlarge my territory, keep me from harm and causing harm. Make me to be a good Stewart over all that you have trusted me with. Help me to recognize every great and effectual door you have placed before me. Enable me Father through your insight to be able to identify every window of opportunity regardless of how it appears before me. Grant me the courage, the will and the grace to believe, trust, obey, serve and receive from you. Lord let this grace, favour and your blessings be pressed down, shaken together and running over in my life that it may spill over into the lives of others for your glory. Help me Father to believe that I have received and I shall have.

Father often times I fail but I'm committed to pursuing your perfection.

# TOTAL DELIVERANCE

Lord, deliver me from past and present hurt, past failures, past and present disappointments and past and present fears.

*"If the Son therefore shall make you free, ye shall be free indeed." (John 8:36 KJV)*

# SEASONS CHANGE

Despite our love for the warmth of summer, we are not able to make it last one moment beyond its set time. Refusing to change the date on the calendar, or neglecting to change to the apparel appropriate for fall doesn't negate the fact that it is what it is. No man, woman, boy or girl possesses the power to stand at the brink of the midnight hour and command that it refuse to come. None of us possess the ability to stand at the curtain of dawn and command the sun not to remove itself from the shadow of the night so that morning doesn't parade across the skies as a moment in time. Fear, the master of deception has no reign over the God ordained purpose that's within. God alone is the commander in chief of times and seasons.

*"Arise, shine; for thy light has come, and the glory of the Lord is risen upon thee." (Isaiah 60:1KJB)*

# A REFRESHING THOUGHT

It's not always going to be the way that it is right now. Things will change; it will get better. This thought brings hope which manifests through a smile. I will praise Him for the changes that will come and they shall be good changes, hope and an expected end.

# TIME BRINGS CHANGES!

Cleanse my heart Oh Lord that I may always be in right standing with you. Let my trust be only in you Oh God, for my help, my deliverance, my blessings, and my inheritance is not just in you but from your hands only. Allow the boundary lines to fall in pleasant places for me.

*"LORD, you alone are my portion and my cup;*
  *you make my lot secure.*

*6 The boundary lines have fallen for me in pleasant places;*
  *surely I have a delightful inheritance." (Psalm 16:5-6NIV)*

Some put their trust in their associations, their accomplishments or in their status quo, but I will trust in the living God! In my immaturity I disliked fire, but in my maturity the presence of fire signifies the opportunity for refinement! I've come to the realization that our perception often times determines our progression. Let your prayers become an action, not just the words that you speak. Time brings changes. I sense a new day dawning!

# WHEN SEASONS ARE CHANGING

Seasons change and when they do none of us are responsible for it because it is a God ordained thing. However, those of us who understand times and seasons know that as they change we must adjust ourselves to accommodate them. Change is a beautiful thing though sometimes the uncertainties of it may cause our faith to waiver inflicting fear upon us. Although fear of the unknown is crippling it cannot and will not supersede the divine will and timing of The Almighty God who is both the author and finisher of our faith and destiny. For some of us the change of a season brings new alignments and assignments which are often times not understood but when there is a direct mandate we **must** comply!

# OUR MOMENTS ARE OUR MESSAGE

The moments of our lives are made up of the places we've been, the people we've met and the experiences we've had. This was and is God's way of building a message. That message is not only shared with those who perhaps were a part of the experiences but additionally it's for those who will later walk a similar road. The message is a reflection of the hope, opportunities and possibilities that are disguised in our challenges.

# MY PRAYER

**Father, today I really need you.**

# STAY FOCUSED!

We must be categorized as lost in order that we may either be found or find our way. My consolation is that God himself knew the way that we would take yet he calls us by that which he does ~ anointed, gifted, teacher, intercessor, worshipper, warrior…

*But he knoweth the way that I take: when he hath tried me, I shall come forth as gold. (Job 23:10KJV)*

# KEEP ON PRESSING!!!!!!

Circumstances sometimes predict hopelessness but it is at times such as these that God's still small voice drowns the very thunderous voice of despair. Things fall apart in order that they may come together. Yes,they do! Everything but God has a beginning and an end! Therefore hard times have an end. Adversity has an end. God has the ability to disrupt the enemy's agenda for your life and mine. He drapes the halls of our minds in the safety of His word shielding us amidst the sometimes chaotic circumstances of life. It won't always be like this. The Lord is in the business of perfection, making all things beautiful in His time. Watch God change it! Sometimes the battle inside rages! The battle takes place at the intersection of where we are and where we long to be. Ministry extends beyond the borders of our emotions, desires and personal agendas. Just beyond the barricades of your spiritual, emotional and physical harassment lays your Eden experience, your Canaan, your blessed place. **Keep on pressing!!!!!!**

## "TODAY I SURRENDER......"

**Lord**, today I surrender.

God calls us to a place of complete surrender and unfeigned forgiveness.

Father helps us to pull down every stronghold and annihilate every opposing force thru the power of Jesus' name. Lord, you are my shield when I feel vulnerable. You are my protection when I feel threatened. You are my rock when I feel as though I'm on shaky ground. Help me to lean on only you when I need to stand strong and resist the temptation to rely on something or someone else. I will lift up praises to you whenever I feel weakened rejoicing in the fact that I have found my strength in you.

Today I accept the fact that I am a new creation in Christ, all things of the past are far behind me now. I don't have to be chained any longer to old mind set, old attitudes, or old ways of doing things. Help me Lord to remember that I am a new creation in every way and to live like it. Help me to remember that you see me through my future and not through my past.

*"Therefore if any man be in Christ, he is a new creature: old things are passed away; behold all things are become new." (2 Corinthians 5:17KJV)*

# BE NOT WEARY.....!

*"And let us not be weary in well doing: for in due season we shall reap, if we faint not."(Galatians 6:9KJV)*

This is our due season! In the name of Jesus the blood of Jesus is against every satanic attack that is launched against us this day and forever more!

# INNER TRUTH

Remember to be true to God and then to yourself. It is only then that you can be effective and true to anything and anyone else. If you are being anything other than whom and what God has instructed you to be you are denying God, yourself and the world.

# "I AM ME"

I refuse to rob myself of who I myself am; that is the very essence of who I am; that which makes me the unique individual that I am. I owe no apology as long as who I am is who God has created me to be. To conform to anything else to be more accommodating to what others think I should be is like trying to be something or someone other than who I am. I am me.

## THE RIGHT MEASUREMENTS

We should never measure ourselves by the yardstick of others; we do ourselves an injustice when we do. We ought to measure our success and accomplishments by the obstacles that we are faced with and the way in which we overcome them to reach where we are. There is greatness on the inside of each of us, but it takes acknowledgement from one's own self.

## A NOTE FROM MY SANCTUARY

*"Dancing is my sanctuary and I don't need any attitude there! No adults allowed! Give me the kids." (Kevvanna Hall)*

You must guard your sanctuary by any means necessary. It's your place and space where trouble, distress and the cares of this life are restricted. It's a place where freedom reigns, a place of solitude, laughter and love. It's that place for which your gifting have made room for you .You are the security that stands at the door and entrance can only be gained by your invitation. Be careful who you entertain there.

## STAY WITHIN GOD'S BOUNDARIES

If you would truly trust God to set the boundaries and stay within the garden where He has planted you it will be okay. You will have it all both wholeness and happiness. Remember that Eve was placed in the garden but God set the boundaries for her. He's doing the same for you. Just trust and obey. When you are about to compromise all that you are meant to be, consider those who only have your example of godliness. There are some persons that have been assigned to you and to whom you have been assigned. Stay in your rightful position.

*"And the LORD God took the man, and put him into the Garden of Eden to dress it and to keep it." (Genesis 2:15KJV)*

# THE BEAUTY OF WHAT THE ALMIGHTY HAS CREATED IS GLORY!

As I sat on the shore overlooking the waters of the sea and gazing at the kaleidoscope of colours parading the sky, I have come to the conclusion that the only description for the beauty of what God has created is GLORY!!!Glory! Glory!

Now I possess a new revelation of David's testimony that the heavens declare the glory of the Lord and the earth is indeed His handiwork. (see Psalm 19:1) For what most of us refer to as nature I describe as the artistic ability of the Almighty God. It stands in a category of its own. To what can it be compared? Even now He's commanding the waters of the sea as the tide rolls out at one hour and in at the next. When I see how He arrays the skies in the early morning I realize that one portion of His creation has the ability to tell many stories all at the same time as the tides listen to the voice of His call to come out and the sun makes its grand entrance amidst the morning clouds; it peers down on the landscape of rocks that was once hidden by the presence of the waters. I see the Lord! As I study the different movement from one body of water it affirms the fact that God has the ability to call forth beauty out of chaos. The fresh air is as the Spirit of God reviving and revitalizing the body of man. What therapy! What priceless medicine! Revival is not exclusive to what we call a church. Revival can take place wherever God chooses. He restores my spirit, body and soul. He is my shepherd.

*"He leads me beside the still waters. He restores my soul….." (Psalm 23:2-3KJV)*

Today I come into agreement with the Spirit of the Lord that it is a good day.

# CONTENTMENT AND JOY IN THE PLACE OF ADVERSITY

Today I saw a crippled young man who was obviously deformed from birth. He walked with imperfections but his face depicted only joy. He was making his journey struggling with his thorn but wearing what appeared to be a permanent smile. He encouraged me, he wore contentment well. In spite the abnormality and the challenges he appeared to be excited about making his journey.

# A SIMPLE PRAYER

Today I acknowledge that God answers even the simplest of prayers. I realize that prayer need not be complicated or multi-faceted. God responds to sincerity. My prayer for the day is simple "Lord, I comply with your perfect will for my life. I want nothing less." Though the prayer was in its simplest form the answers came in droves. God is amazing.

**"God, can you please help me? That covers everything I need to say to you. Thank you for caring so much."**

# PURPOSE IS BORN OUT OF PAIN.

I woke up one morning with the thought that where I was wasn't where I wanted to be. I wasn't happy with mediocrity, frustration, lack, the struggles and all else that accompanied them. These were not my desires. I once heard a man say that the worst time to eat is when we are extremely hungry. His reasoning was that at these times we are desperate and will eat whatever is before us. We make decisions out of desperation saying and doing things that in the long term could be to our detriment. I wish not to depart this life without fulfilling my purpose. I wish not that my dreams, desires and purpose which I refer to as my spiritual baby die in the birthing canal which is to be interpreted as a miscarriage. Neither do I wish to abort that which I carry. At times I feel as though I am strangling in my own blood or haemorrhaging. "Lord, save me, save that which You have implanted in me!" This is a cry that denotes weakness, frailty, vulnerability and desperation. I know that there must be a better way but the challenge is to find it. It is obvious that desire alone is insufficient. A life that is lived without purpose is one that is spent in much frustration, resentment, pain and anguish.

**For as the body without the spirit is dead, so faith without works is dead also. (James 2:26KJV)**

# GIVING BIRTH

Pain comes; we push, then comes the gift of life in the form of our baby ~ **LIFE**

# SAYING NO TO OTHERS CAN SOMETIMES MEAN SAYING YES TO GOD'S AGENDA!

# ACCESS GRANTED

There is a place and space that I have exclusive access to no matter where I am and who's around.

# TAKING A BREAK

We have become too busy for the simple and essential things of life.

# NEW THINKING

The thinking that has brought you this far is not the thinking that is going to take you any further. It has to be a new thought!

*Instead, let the Spirit renew your thoughts and attitudes.....* *(Ephesians 4:23NLT)*

**My Husband once advised that I learn to value what I do.** Perhaps you undervalue what it is that God has blessed your hands to do.

"Dwight Brice"

DESTINATION~ in the will of God be girded with truth (the word) and position yourself in prayer these will assist as you encounter momentary turbulence. Trust and Obey and you will arrive safely!!!!!!

# THIS IS THE HOUR TO FOLLOW THE SPIRIT OF GOD WITH PRECISION AND WITHOUT RESERVATION

Father, in the name of JESUS CHRIST, THE LAMB OF GOD, by THE SPIRIT of God I cancel the plans of every satanic agent!!!!!!!! On the authority of the name of Jesus I dispatch the angels of God, and the Spirit of The Living God to hijack permanently and foil the enemies plans for my life, the lives of my sons and daughters,family, friends, neighbours and my community members.' I plead the blood of Jesus to every case and every situations!!!!! I call forth my Jehovah Sabboath to wage war against the host of hell on behalf of every ambassador for Christ and everything and everyone connected to them. Lord seal our lives, our destiny, our children, our homes, our marriages our resources our integrity our weapons of warfare our country our community and our health with the blood of Jesus! Spirit of The Living God intercede on our behalf covering every area that we have missed with the blood of Jesus Christ, our saviour, our deliverer, our healer, our way maker ! Lord we say yes to your assignment for our lives. Stand guard oh Lord arm us to stand against the wiles, the trickery, the delusion, the agenda and the attacks of the enemy in Jesus ' name. Father in the name of Jesus dry up the grounds and the root of every evil tree and seed planted by the enemy for your name sake. Grant us gracious Father the grace to stand and go forth in the power of the Holy Ghost. Let the Holy Ghost come upon us Father even as the day of Pentecost that revival, restoration, salvation, deliverance, healing and wholeness may come out of your sanctuary for our good and your glory. Father we say thank you!!!!! Set our faces as flint and our feet as hind's feet!!!Gird our loins with the truth, Thy word oh Lord is truth. Let truth prevail over our lives in Jesus' name. We REBUKE THE SPIRIT OF DISTRUCTION IN JESUS' NAME!!! Hallelujah!!!!Amen ~ so let it be! We acknowledge Father, that this is the hour to follow your leading with precision and without reservation.

Father I seal these prayers in the blood of Jesus. In Jesus' name I come against backlash, retaliation and vengeance!!!!

Lord, let the sword of your Spirit which is the word protrude from my spirit and my mouth and from the spirit and mouth of your ambassadors in the four corners of the earth piercing the spirit realm in Jesus' name!

# ENJOY YOUR LIQUID SUNSHINE

"Today is supposed to be my beach day.... it's raining hard outside". L (Wilna Joseph)

Sometimes God gives what is needed instead of what is wanted. Sometimes He chooses to first provide what is needed and then later gives us what we wanted with His blessings. Delay doesn't mean denied. Perhaps He's got other plans for you for right now. J Enjoy the liquid sunshine!

# THE CALL TO GO

Sometimes the call to go doesn't come at what we may consider a convenient time. Nevertheless, the mandate must be obeyed!

# THE PLACE OF REMEMBRANCE

It is always good to visit the foundation of our faith; it is the place of passion where we immersed ourselves in intimacy with God. It's a place from which the fountain of healing, deliverance and breakthrough flows. It is where we were so interwoven into the presence of God. The place where we learnt to press, to worship and to wait for our God to invade the prison of our brokenness and liberate us through His power, His grace, His mercy and His love. It is the place of assurance where our God made it known to us that ALL IS WELL!

**Father, I thank you for the place of remembrance. Thank you for reminding me that Jesus Christ is the same yesterday, today and forever. Thank you for leaving open the door that leads to the place where you nourished me with your goodness.**

# TODAY I PRAY

Lord of the Breakthrough go before me today!!!!! Breakdown every satanic wall!!!!! Oppose every satanic agent seen and unseen, Nullify every demonic device, breakup every evil confederacy against me, my family, my friends and the body of Christ at large in Jesus' name. Present us faultless and blameless and dress us in an excellent spirit, gird our loins with truth, enlighten our understanding and instruct us in the way we should go. Holy Spirit intercede on our behalf according to the will of our Heavenly Father, spiritually sanitize our homes, workplaces, marriages, community, schools, justice system and every other system. Purge us Dear Lord! Go before us and be behind us with fire, hide us in your pavilion in Jesus' name. Thank you for good success and allowing us to possess the fruit of the Spirit. Grant us the will, desire and the ability through the Holy Ghost to be agents of Change and Ambassadors of the Kingdom of Light! Amen~ so let it be. Stand guard over the words you have spoken to us and guard this prayer in Jesus' name. In The name of Jesus, I COME AGAINST BACKLASH, RETALIATION AND VENGEANCE!!!! Lord lay your axe to the root of every evil tree planted in our lives. Destroy evil seed, tree and fruit that was planted in Jesus' name. Let the Law of substitution work on our behalf today even as it did for Mordecai in Jesus' name. Let the Hemans, Jezebels and Pharaohs meet their faith according to the seeds sown in Jesus' name. Bless us Lord, keep us from harm and from causing Harm in Jesus' name and again I say Amen!

**Lord of the Breakthrough!**

# OPERATION OVERRIDE!

OVER-RIDE!!!!!!!!!!!!!!! I hear in my Spirit OVER-RIDE! Ain't no stopping me now; God's in the driver's seat! Every negative thing written, spoken or suggested that is contrary to God's will for my life will be overridden! Access granted! I hear the chains falling, I sense the atmosphere shifting, it's turning around, and there will be glory after this!!!!! Let the church say ~~~~~~AMEN!!!!!!!!!!! ~ SO LET IT BE!!!!

# FLOATING ON WATER

In as much as I expect not to be understood yet still it is my desire to be understood. Life's challenges are often times overwhelming resulting in our actions being unseemly.

God drew my attention to an individual attempting to float on water. The water will either support you or it will overflow you causing you to sink. The Spirit of God advised that when we relax and breathe we tend to float however, anxiety and panic causes us to sink.

We can allow our circumstances to carry us toward our purpose or we can act anxiously towards them and sink aborting our purpose.

# THE VALLEY EXPERIENCES

He is God enough to set up His throne even in our valley experiences. A valley is defined as low point or condition. Valleys are often found between ranges of hills or mountains. Sometimes as believers we find ourselves in the meandering of the valley of the shadows of darkness. It is there that the enemy comes in as a flood to buffet us seeking to force us to compromise our posture in God. In the valley we are often vulnerable because we are closed in by life's hills and mountains. In the valley God reveals Himself as Yeshua. Yeshua in Hebrew is verbal derivative from "to rescue", "to deliver". When we address our heavenly Father as Yeshua it is a deliberate, desperate cry for help. Yeshua stands guard over those that are His even as a shepherd in the valley, comforting us with His rod and staff.

# THE BIRTHING PROCESS

The birthing process is preceded by rigid labour pains and embodied in vigorous work.

# THE EFFECTUAL, REVERENT PRAYER ......

For most of us prayer is the recitation of words we have committed to memory as opposed to words that flows from the heart. There is a difference between head knowledge and heart knowledge! I had gotten up and had started to pray, so I thought. As I began, I heard the Holy Spirit ask "Are you praying from the head or from your heart"? I immediately stopped and thought about it! He began to say that so many of us don't see the results of prayer because we have prayed not from a heart of full conviction or belief but from a head of knowledge. I quickly repented! I now understand why I walked in the spirit of fear but was saying "God is our refuge and strength, a very present help in trouble" (Psalm 46:1 KJV) Though these words hold power the demonstration of that power comes when they are released from the heart to the lips to the atmosphere but the power of these words lie dormant when released from the head to the lips to the atmosphere. We declare from the lips but not from the heart and as a result we see no manifestation of the dynamos power that the word of God possess'.

# THE GIFT

I wish to daily give a gift that is priceless. It's not found on a shelf or a luxurious boutique. It is the love, joy, peace and kindness that are found only in Knowing the Heavenly Father. I wish to motivate, to encourage, to uplift and to inspire.

I want to know that minds are being transformed, burdens are being uplifted, yokes are being destroyed, and hope is restored. I wish that broken hearts are mended, spirits are stirred and renewed, blinded eyes they must see, captives they too be made free! I want to know that God is being glorified, problems are being rectified, God's people are being sanctified, hell is being depopulated and God's kingdom is being enlarged. These are the gifts that keep on giving.

# MY PRAYER.

**Father God, Please give me a precise plan to get from where I am to where you need me to be.**

**Father, when you give me this plan give me also the courage, grace and favour to execute it and**

**Grant me not only success but also fulfilment~ Amen**

# GLADIATOR IN STILETTOS

I'm a real woman with real struggles, fighting real wars, manoeuvring through life's obstacles in wedges and stilettos. I guess witness must not be without credence. Instead of makeup I use prayer, praise, worship and warfare to cover my wounds and scars. I'm broken but I'm armed and dangerous, running through troops and leaping over walls, treading on serpents and scorpions with a face as flint and feet as hinds.

I'm trying to polarize the works of my flesh, eulogize my God, and harmonize my spirit with His word.

Beauty for ashes is what I've been promised.

*1The Spirit of the Sovereign L*ORD *is on me,*
*because the L*ORD *has anointed me*
*to proclaim good news to the poor.*
*He has sent me to bind up the brokenhearted,*
*to proclaim freedom for the captives*
*and release from darkness for the prisoners,* ᵃ
*2to proclaim the year of the L*ORD*'s favor*
*and the day of vengeance of our God,*
*to comfort all who mourn, and provide for those who grieve in Zion—*
*to bestow on them a crown of beauty*
*instead of ashes,*
*the oil of joy*
*instead of mourning,*
*and a garment of praise*
*instead of a spirit of despair.*
*They will be called oaks of righteousness,*
*a planting of the L*ORD
*for the display of his splendor.(Isaiah 61:1-3 NIV)*

# INSPIRED BY YOU ~ TERRI ANTONIO ROLLE

An amazing woman of God once said to me "Pay attention to your calling or you will forever be uncomfortable!"

So today, tomorrow and forever I vow to DEDICATE all of me to that which God has called me to. In doing so I surrender totally and I acknowledge that I will make a conscious, consistent effort to comply and submit to He who has called me. I therefore give my complete attention to my time, talents, gifts and abilities being totally reliant upon The Spirit of The Living God who is the giver of every good and perfect gift. I solely depend upon Him to complete the good work that He alone has begun. I therefore decree and declare that I will write and publish every book that is within me, I will sing every song and sound of praise that my vocal cords were ordained to project into the atmosphere. I will pray every prayer that my heart and spirit are instructed to. I will preach every sermon and make manifest by the grace of God ALL that He has purposed in His heart concerning me.

# I LOVE TO SHARE~

There is a system at work in the world that equates sharing to distributing ones goods and leaving one's self depleted. However the order of God defies this very idea.

When we share what we have plowing the soil of the hearts of men we distribute love, joy, peace, hope and the confidence that God is well able. When we plant a seed it produces a tree which bears fruit that again produces seeds and those seeds produce the very same cycle again carrying on the cycle of seed, time and harvest. When we tap into this system we unlock heaven's bounty causing the unleashing of an inexhaustible supply of heaven's goodness, grace, love and perfection.

## ARISE!

Woman/Man of God arise! Arise, woman/man of God! You know your God. He is no stranger to you or you to Him. Because you know your God great works are inevitable!

## THERE IS LIFE RIGHT WHERE YOU ARE.

I've seen flowers growing from within rocks. What is so amazing is that the rock doesn't depict the ideal conditions for such a thing. However, there is a revelatory message in this. That plant is an irrefutable indication that the God we serve grants us the grace to grow in the midst of adversity or one might say in some of the most adverse conditions. Soil is garnished with the nutrients required for a healthy plant yet the wall made out of rocks were adorned with some of the most beautiful greenery. That tells me that God gives us what we need to defy the very order of nature and produce right where we are in some of the most abrasive, hostile and callous environments.

## A WAY IN THE WILDERNESS

Often times when we refer to a wilderness it denotes a painful experience, an emptiness or barrenness. When one speaks of a wilderness experience it generally speaks to a time of stagnation, an unproductive place or a place of punishment. Contrary to this connotation we often fail to associate a wilderness with anything good, profitable or productive. Until today I have also failed to associate a wilderness with anything positive. This speaks volumes of the fact that many of us fail to see things for all that they really are. When we talk about our wilderness we speak for one aspect only, hardship.

What about the wilderness that causes us to yield to God's original plan, agenda or purpose? That state of being where we did not add to or subtract from what God said about us. The place that denotes God's unmodified will for you and me.

What if we allow Holy Spirit to enlighten our dark understanding for a moment to all that the wilderness really represents; will our cry be the same as before "Lord, get me out of my wilderness experience!" Or will it be "Lord, take me to my wilderness so that I can know who I really am." Often times to understand a thing we need to visit its place of origination. The foundation reveals and holds the weight of all that stands upon it.

# GOD WANTS US HEALED AND WHOLE!

# RISE UP WOMAN OF GOD RISE UP!

# THEY THAT KNOW THEIR GOD SHALL DO GREAT EXPLOITS!

# YOU KNOW GOD! HE IS NO STRANGER TO YOU!

I love to share! According to the natural order of things when we share what we have it means we are spreading it to others and perhaps diminishing our supply. However the order of God defies that very same order. When we share the system is reversed and we are actually on the gaining end. In sharing we are scattering seeds of joy, hope, love, peace and all that pertains to life and godliness. The ploughing of the fields of the hearts of men produces a harvest of return that far outweighs our scattering. Each seed produces a tree and each tree produces fruit and that fruit produces seed and the seed repeats that very same cycle hence our lives are filled with heaven's bounty and earth's treasures. Selah! ~ To Terri Rolle ~ my inspiration because she has a heart of gold that listens, encourages and loves.

# MAMMOTH OF A TASK ~ SOMETIMES THE SOLUTION IS AN ACT OF OBEDIENCE, *THE CALL TO OBEY.*

There were days when what I faced seemed a mammoth of a task and I would say to The Lord "where do I begin?" I simply did not know where to begin so I'd sit and dread what I saw before me. One day in the midst of rehearsing the routine line, "I don't know where to begin" the Holy Spirit commanded me to "HALT!" He said "do not say that you don't know where to begin." I've said that so many times before. He advised me to just begin. Everything around me seemed cluttered bedrooms and all. Somehow it seemed if I could rid the house of the clutter I would free up the clutter in my mind and heart. As I glanced over both rooms the Holy Spirit turned my attention to the bed. He advised me to begin right there. The bed sat in the middle of the room, I obeyed. It was to me a small start in the midst of the enormous one but nonetheless I did; it took my attention of the entire task and focused on one portion at a time.

In the midst of the cleaning and discarding I found an old receipt book. Holding it in my hand I glanced over the room looking at what I accomplished. To me it didn't seem like much. At that very moment in a still small voice I heard the words "you began." I agreed. As I turned my attention back to that old receipt book I was led to glance through the pages and I found the following words:

October 19th 2013

*I am a covenant keeping God. My word is established forever. I have called you to the circumcision of the flesh. Once the flesh is circumcised you will receive what I the Lord has promised. I call you into remembrance of April 9th on your bed of affliction, it was there that again you Tharan Anneth Gardiner Brice cut covenant with I the Lord, your God, the true and living God who is and forever will be a consuming fire even unto the wicked. I have called, chosen and redeemed your life from destruction. Thou art mine! I will call my judgement and fury on anything and anyone that stands in the way of this covenant. I The Lord have spoken and I will repay, yea, for I the Lord have drawn you out of many deep, tumultuous and even treacherous waters and have loved you. Yet you refuse to accept that you are the blessed of me the Lord. I have loved and cared for you, yet still you so desire the love of man and their acceptance. You have allowed this desire to wound your spirit man whom I have redeemed and bought with the price of the shed blood of my Son your Lord and Saviour Jesus the Christ. I rebuke you daughter because I love you. Thou art mine!! Harken unto me, unto my voice lest you die. I am the Lord thy God, thy maker, the redeemer, your first husband. I married you calling you unto myself when many have rejected you. Thou art mine. I have favoured you. You are mine, yet you behave as do a bastard child. Hast thou not heard or believed that you are mine? Must my Son be crucified again for you to believe what I have said? Rest in me. Yea, I love thee and do chastise thee because of my love for thee. I will show you my loving kindness but you must refuse to rebel in your heart. I am the true and living God who is the same yesterday, today and forever. Thou art mine. I have called thee, I have chosen thee and yes I have loved and do love thee my daughter. Thou art mine!!*

Now and forever the key to our deliverance is total obedience to God and what He says. When we obey even the mammoth becomes minute.

**When The Father looks upon me and all that I do or say I'd like for His response to be "Calvary was worth it!"**

*...17To You I shall offer a sacrifice of thanksgiving, And call upon the name of the LORD. 18I shall pay my vows to the LORD, Oh may it be in the presence of all His people, 19In the courts of the LORD'S house, In the midst of you, O Jerusalem. Praise the LORD! (Psalm 116:17-18) NASB*

# ANSWERING THE CALL OF SELF-ACCEPTANCE, SELF-APPRECIATION AND SELF-LOVE.

I often think of what I have not done rather than what I have. I realize that I have paid so much attention to the negativity in my life giving no place to enjoy the making of all the wonderful possibilities. I believe that this was and is the devil's tool. Whilst talking with the Lord revelation pierced through the curtains of my understanding. God wants us to spend more time looking at the positive side of life. In the still small voice of the Comforter (The Holy Spirit) came the words "embrace yourself, start appreciating what you have done and where you are rather than grieving over where you've been or where you think you should be... Give yourself the credit that you would so often give to others." In that moment I decided that I wanted to stop "beating up" myself. You see like many of you I've done that for such a long time. I joined in with the ambush that was set up by the enemy to assault me. Today that ends I'm on my side regardless of who isn't. I support me. I believe in me. I believe in the assignment and call of God that is on my life. By the grace of God I will not be distracted or detoured from my assignment or my assigned place.

# GOD'S AGENDA

I believe that at the point of our conception and even before God has a plan for our lives. A part of that plan consists of that which He has called us to or predestined for us. Many of us spend time wondering through life attempting to chart our own course disregarding the directives of The Holy Spirit giving way to much frustration, vexation and often times destruction. God, our creator has the master plan for our lives. He knows the ultimate purpose for which we were born; in fact regardless of the agendas of your parents God's intent was purposed filled. Rather than spend our days wondering and making erroneous decisions we should opt to consult our Heavenly Father for He has created each of us with an exclusive manual. You were born one of a kind even if you shared your mother's womb with another. You were yet still uniquely designed by God. There is no need to imitate someone else. You were born to be distinctively you. Stop and listen for and to the Holy Spirit's instructions. Allow Him to download your true identity. God's plans were authentically purposed with you in mind; submit to His call. It is only when we acquiesce to God's plans for our lives that purpose and destiny collides on our behalf bringing forth the manifestation of God's perfect will and placing us in the centre of it. There is a void in the life of every individual who disregards God's call. Some people spend a lifetime trying to fill that void with everything else but that which is able to succour it. The answer is simply "yes Lord!" We spend so much time doing everything else but that which we were born to do. I was once guilty.

**"Father, grant me both the will and the desire to give you a complete yes."**

*But Samuel replied: "Does the LORD delight in burnt offerings and sacrifices as much as in obeying the LORD? To obey is better than sacrifice, and to heed is better than the fat of rams. (1Samuel 15:22NIV)*

# IT IS A GREAT WORK! (12:05 PM JANUARY 31ST 2010)

**It is** a great work but it is unfinished. The fullness of its beauty may not be seen by the naked untrained eyes. Perhaps only the Architect, he who has designed it knows the full revelation of its beauty. Those whom he has graced with a preview of the completed work only see but a phase of its splendour. During the building process its edges are rough and may be seen as an eye sore. Unfinished, unpolished, loose ends, nakedness and rubble is the present state of that which is to come. ~ a reflection of Heaven's splendour and the King's glory!

The prophecy and the gift stand as the architectural drawing which is God's promise. The work that goes into it is not known or understood by many; however, the finished product will impact many. Many will reap the benefits though they may have no knowledge or appreciation for the process of its erection.

*So do not throw away your confidence; it will be richly rewarded. You need to persevere so that when you have done the will of God, you will receive what he has promised. (Hebrews 10:35-36NIV)*

What is the promise? It is the manifestation of the prophecy and the utilization of the gifts to the honour and glory of Him who has not only begun the work but also completed and established it!

The place of process is never comfortable.

*But the pot he was shaping from the clay was marred in his hands; so the potter formed it into another pot, shaping it as seemed best to him.(Jeremiah 18:4NIV)*

## FREEDOM.....

Some of us have been held hostage by the terrorist known as fear. Fear has hijacked our faith attempting to recondition us to the point of denying both the power and the word of God resulting in many persons living below God's standard and ultimately outside of His perfect will.

When the power of God comes with His anointing we are set free. However, when we neglect to submit to the overhauling of our minds and hearts through the word of God and the Spirit of God we continue to subconsciously choose to live in bondage relinquishing our rights to the heritage of freedom.

# SOMETIMES, MOST TIMES THE GIFTING IS WITHIN US. HARD TIMES ARE MEANT TO BRING THEM OUT!

### *Freedom~ the Option~ the balm of forgiveness*

Imagine being imprisoned by emotions and life's challenging experiences. This can leave us crippled spiritually, physically, emotionally and financially. Consider being held in such a position for a very long time and then being given the key that can set you free. However, in order to experience this freedom you would be required to utilize these keys given to you. Forgiveness serves as the key that can unlock many of our prisons. To forgive is to strangle the weeds of anger and bitterness which can cause grievous harm if left alone. Forgiveness is the only cure for rage and resentment. It involves giving up the desire to get even. IT serves as spiritual sanitation and freedom from captivity. I am a firm believer that to forgive is to acquit those who may have wronged us of the offence thereby setting them free not from God's judgement but our own. I have come to realize that many persons opt to stay bound simply because they find it impossible to let go of an offence. In fact they chose to hold fast to the desire to make the offender pay. To forgive is to open two prison doors at once both yours and the offender's. Often times we may find it more painful to forgive because it entails setting our offenders free. Un-forgiveness is the most fortified prison bars. Its foundation is anger and resentment. Why are you still bound? Leave judgement and justice to God!

## A NOTE FROM MY HEART:

Tonight I stood in the face of the truth. Behind sickness, sorrow, deep seethed anger, resentment and discontentment is the spirit of un-forgiveness and rebelliousness against God. Forgiveness is to assume the posture of submission and total surrender to God.

Freedom to live, laugh and love ~ Forgiveness

Un-forgiveness is a toxin that poisons our very existence. It eats away at the very fibre of qualities that fashions us after the likeness of God. Eventually it causes us to become that which we may have once despised and could even result in ill health.

When we choose to hold on to an offence the end result is like giving the offender both hammer and nails to lock us away in a prison with bars of anger, resentment, frustration and perhaps hatred. We deny ourselves the liberty to operate in love, joy and peace. On the contrary, when we choose to forgive the offender no longer holds power over us.

When one chooses to live a life that reflects the love of God forgiveness becomes second nature. It is treated as a way of life and is not predicated on the conditions or circumstances one may encounter. In the "Our Father Prayer" we are made to understand that we are required to forgive in order that we ourselves may be forgiven. Jesus illustrates the perfect example of unconditional forgiveness when He requested that his father forgive those who had offended him to the point of crucifixion. To have a forgiving heart equates to both abundant and eternal life. It is being afforded the privilege of displaying God's splendour and showing forth His glory whilst giving life and light to others. When we forgive we are free to live, laugh and love.

# WHY DO WE WORRY? ~ HE COVERS ME!

Sometimes life's challenges attempts to back us into a corner and overwhelm us as the darkness of midnight. It is important to know how and when to withdraw and allow the Lord to lead you beside still waters that our soul may be restored. Look at the birds of the air and the lilies of the field, they neither toil nor spin but the Lord provides. Why do we worry?

I look at the trees on the outside; how tall and strong they are! Nobody waters or fertilizes them yet they possess the fortitude that they do. "The Lord provides!" He arrays them with the beauty of colour, strength, seed, fruit, leaves and limbs. They are shade, food and shelter to both man and beast. They are indeed the manifestation of the grace, love, peace, shelter and provision of God~ *(For in the time of trouble he shall hide me in his pavilion: in the secret of his tabernacle shall he hide me; he shall set me up upon a rock. Psalms 27:5).KJV*

He covers me as a bride decked for her groom on her wedding day. He covers me as the skies drape the four corners of the earth. He waters my soul with gladness as the waters fills portions of the earth seeping into places that may forever remain unseen. He comforts me as do the breast of a mother do a new born babe. He fascinates me as a lover does the one he or she so loves. He pardons me as do grace a sinner. He holds me when by my strength I do fall. He loves me beyond measure. He answers when I call.

In the midst of turmoil He creates the rhythm to which I can dance. ~ *(You have turned my mourning into joyful dancing. You have taken away my clothes of mourning and clothed me with joy... Psalm 30:11NLT).*

## TRUTH IS

*The truth is all my life from as far back as I can remember I've searched for love .There was a deep seethed desire to be loved. The misunderstanding of this love that I longed for led me in pursuit of the love that was tangible; this was my only understanding of what I had longed for. Until now I thought it was that I longed to be a wife, to love and be loved. I was in search of a love that would fill the abyss I* barley understood. I was clueless of the fact that I spent a great portion of my life looking for a love that I've always had. I couldn't identify or appreciate it. Truth is I was searching for God! I spent so many days in what I thought was the quest of a relationship that would pacify this longing only to be disappointed, rejected, misunderstood and taken advantage of.

## VALIDATION

Being rejected by man has qualified me to be chosen by God! He was wounded and bruised that I might receive right standing and forgiveness.

## I DARE NOT!!!!!!

I dare not take the grace of God for granted!!!! I dare not in arrogance look down on others because I've found hope and strength in the power of the Gospel of Jesus Christ and in having intimate relationship with Him. I dare not boast or scorn others in self-Righteousness for it is God who has given me the will and the ability to do well. I dare not wield the authority of His word as a personal rod of judgment and condemnation but rightly dividing His word allowing vengeance to be His and victory to be mine.

## I'D RATHER.........

I'd rather know that I did and I didn't have to than to know that I didn't and I needed to.

# THE ESSENCE OF TRUE TREASURE

*Why do we heap up treasures for ourselves here on earth where thieves break in and steal and elements destroy? For a very long time we were thought to believe that our greatest treasures were the things that we possess like our homes, vehicles, titles, children or spouses. However, our greatest treasure is that which cannot be bought with that which is corruptible. It is that which we so often overlook and take for granted. Our greatest possession outside of a relationship with Christ Jesus is a sound mind (peace of mind).When we wake up each morning clothed in our right mind that's a blessing. When we possess the peace of God in our hearts and mind that's prosperity. If we lose our homes we can get another, if we lose a spouse or a child as painful as it is we may gain others; if we lose a job that too can be replaced. When we possess a sound mind and God's peace we can attain anything and withstand all things!*

*For what **does** it **profit** a **man** to gain the whole world and forfeit his soul? (Matt 8:36) NIV*

*Our soul is the essence of who we really are. It cohabits with our mind. The enemy will occupy and set up a mortgage in our minds without the empowerment that comes from knowing, understanding and respecting this truth.*

**Father, help me not for one day take for granted the miracle of grace that is wrapped up in a sound mind filled with your peace. In the name of Jesus stand guard around the perimeters of our minds, set up your word as stakes that would hedge us in from the attacks of the enemy. Amen!**

# LIVE IN READINESS!!!

*Christmas was fast approaching and we've been having some challenges coming to an agreement with what was necessary and of course with the timing with which things should have been done. The tension was so thick it had draped not only the walls of our home but it also covered the walls of our hearts with it cold callous grip. He was frustrated and so was I. The signs of it manifested in every way possible .I sat and looked around just gazing at what seemed more of a war zone and chaos rather than a home that actually housed a family that supposedly loved each other. The angry words matched the chaotic state of each room. I began to question God. "What do I do now?" "How do I fix this?" "Why should I?"*

*I sat to the computer and asked the Lord to convince me. Here's what happened:*

*I had more questions than a curious toddler. My body felt as though it was taking on the toxic environment. In a still small voice I heard the words "make peace" it's so much easier. I took the time to consider the two opposing efforts.*

*"Why not pretend that I Jesus was coming by for a visit", in fact He often does. Then came the other question~ If Jesus were to take on a physical form and pay the house a visit would you be pleased with the state He found it in? Would you say "we were at odds so I chose to do nothing"? I suddenly felt the motivation that I had seemed to have lost. Some may call it pretence. I consider it the reconditioning of the mind.*

*I suddenly had the desire and the will to live in readiness. If I lived each day expecting to Host and house The King of Glory I realize that I would never wait to be motivated, appreciated, celebrated or*

*assisted by anyone else. Choosing to live in readiness made living*
*with the challenges a whole lot easier.*


*Dear Father,*

*There is so much I need and want to say to you but I just can't seem to*
*get the words out verbally. I remember years ago when I used to write*
*you letters. It was a language that was just between us that I was so*
*sure you understood and accepted. I figured since I was challenged in*
*what others consider the normal way of praying I'd talk to you the way*
*I used to. So here I am at it flows. Thanks for allowing me to come to*
*you like this. This takes me way back! Although that was a painful*
*place it was a good place because it was there that we grew so intimate.*
*So much is happening right now, all of which you are aware of. Before*
*I started writing you I felt so far away. Now I fell much closer. Thank*
*you for loving me and understanding me and allowing me to come*
*"Just as I am."*

*I need you to know that I do love you. You are my strength, my comfort,*
*my confidence, my song, my dance, my laughter and my everything.*
*Please don't allow me to have my own way. I realize that your way is*
*so much better for me. I need you. Please strengthen me, forgive me and*
*cleanse me. Make my heart a place where you delight to dwell. Make*
*my life, my home, my work, my marriage, my business, my family and*
*my witness a place where you find delight and pleasure. Cuddle me*
*the way you used to when I was alone rejected and afraid. I know that*
*I've grown a bit and you've given me some of the gifts that I've asked*
*of you like my husband and all but Father I'm really messed up and I*
*need you. I want so much to please you and to have a beautiful life but*
*it all seems such a struggle right now.*

*I miss the way we used to commune. I want to talk to you more. I know that in as much as it would be your delight it would be beneficial to me and to those that you have called me to. Can you please empty me of the toxins of sin in its various forms? Take away the hurt, disappointment, anger, hostility, frustration, vexation, un-forgiveness, disappointment, rejection and all the other gifts that the enemy has given. Help me to love, trust, obey, believe and serve again. Assure me again of your love, faithfulness, forgiveness and presence.*

*Teach me and enable me through the work of The Holy Spirit to live a spirit filled life in a way that brings you glory and draws others to you. Help me to begin again. Set me free from the yokes and burdens that the enemy wills to destroy me. Give me a voice again, not one that seeks to hurt or cause others pain but one that brings you glory and brings deliverance to your people. Lord but first give me deliverance from the snares of the fowler and noisome pestilence. Lord heal me .Heal my husband, my marriage, my children my business, my family. Give us the ability to bring this healing to others.*

**The lord allowed me to become aquatinted with rejection so that the fear of being rejected wouldn't keep me silent. I have been gifted through every hurt and betrayal! I sense it even when it seems hidden. He didn't give the gift for us to throw tantrums; the insight was not for me to act out but instead to PRAY OUT!**

## WAKE UP!!!!!!!!!!!!

*Wake up oh slumbering giants! Father, empty me of every type of invaluable weight or cargo. Father, empty me of negative thoughts ideas opinions self-image. Cause me to begin to live holistic and productive! Cause every gift in me the known and unknown to answer the call that* is upon my life that is your call. Cause every investment you have made in me to bear fruit after its kind.

## DAMSEL ARISE!!!!

Ladies you don't have to be little miss muffet! In fact she never really existed! She's a part of what's known as fairy-tale. However I don't think she became so well-known because she ate curds and whey. Little Miss muffet was probably minding her own business when the spider came along and frightened her away. She allowed him in her space and permitted him to cause her to abandon her position, her possession and perhaps herself while she did nothing about it .She accepted fear which was the gift he gave and with fear she hopelessly ran away. Don't imitate her! Get up and do something! Fight to maintain who you are! You are beautiful, fearfully and wonderfully made! You are strong, you possess the ability to carry life and give birth through pain. You deserve happiness! Christ came that you may have life and have it more abundantly. He thinks good thoughts towards you not evil ones. He wills that you have hope and a future. Live!!!!!!! Talitha cumi-damsel arise!

## STOP!!!!!!!!

Stop waiting for someone else to make it happen! Paint your God given vision on the canvas of time and they will see it and run with it or they will maintain their position and stand at ease. Stop waiting on their support or approval trust what God has placed in you and on you. Some things will never change until you change by becoming the change. If you would synchronize your thoughts words and actions with that of the Holy Spirit of God you will not only accomplish but you will win!!!!! You must win!!!!! When you were alone you relied totally upon me and made things happen; now it seems your idea of trust in me has somewhat changed! Fortify yourself in me and through me again!

## SOUL CRY

I feel like Moses ready to Strike this rock but I'm reminded of the fact that there are consequences for the smallest degree of disobedience. I'd drape myself in Elijah's mantle that he wore to call down fire from heaven but I have some loved ones that would be seared in its flame and I too because of my old nature who fights to dominate at this very moment. So I choose the words of my broken weary yet strong and submissive Saviour I cry Eli Eli lama Sabatini!!!! I carefully chose to use the cries of the psalmist David, a man after God's own heart "show me a token for Good that they which hate me may see it and be ashamed because thou has helped and comforted me."

## FATHER............!

I stand at the threshold of "the new ". I must make a conscious effort to either answer the call or move forward in a quick progressive March or continue to mind the obstacles and challenges opting to mark time in frustration resentment and procrastination. It is by no means a walk in the park but it's like swimming against a raging currant. The human emotions untamed are indeed a bottomless rebellious sea. One must yield to God to overcome it! Father, send help out of your sanctuary so that I may overcome!

# THE SUDDENLY

When God gives you the suddenly your known position and condition changes instantaneously!!!! It could cause you to even look foolish because your physical man may still be trying to explain the last known state of affairs. Don't get caught in frustration, acknowledge your presence in a Kairos moment; celebrate and embrace the miracle of the suddenly of God which is for your good and His glory!!!! There are times God releases the answers to prayers instantly while we are yet asking and we fail to acknowledge that the answer has come because we are still in 'the waiting' when God has already ushered us into 'the receiving'! Satan will always try to get us distracted! His plan is to get you to look away so that he can kill steal or destroy. Normally he uses offence to distract you from seeing your blessing, your victories and Gods power!

# THE ROOT MUST DIE!!!!

The root must die!!!!!!! Father, visit our past and that of our forefathers, destroy the root of every generational curse in Jesus' name! You're God enough for yesterday today and forever. Uproot every evil seed, the trees and its fruits! Severe every ungodly soul-tie and evict every foul spirit in Jesus' name! Release your anointing to destroy the yokes and remove the burdens, send your consuming fire to spiritually sanitize, cause us to no longer deny the power of godliness. Heal us, deliver us and set us free that we may walk worthy of the vocation to which we have been called. Hedge us in with the protection of your presence so that the serpent will not bite! Infuse our bloodline with your righteousness! Cause us by thy grace to pursue your heart and your kingdom! Thine Oh Lord is the kingdom, the power, the glory, the victory and the majesty! Amen!

# I KNOW WHERE YOU ARE

*This morning as I prayed The Holy Spirit reminded me of the following: I know where you are, what you need and what's happening around you. I have the power to change it today, right now if I wish to. You must trust me and my promise to you that all things are working together for your good and my glory. If I permit the situation to persist you must rest in my promise that it is working for your good. I've come to the realization that like the word declares in 2 Timothy 3:5 we know a form of godliness but deny the power thereof. My spirit acknowledges this power but my flesh debates, denies and rebels against it! My flesh must be convicted, convinced and corrected. It is only then will changes begin to manifest even if it initiates internally. I realize that I need the refiner's fire. If I am exempted I will mismanage any promotion or promise given by Abba. Once I've learnt to rest in this revelation, the transitional process will be less painful and frustration will no longer be able to impede my progression.*

# SOLITARY MOMENTS

*I believe that there are times when we must step away from everything and everyone and ask the Lord "are you pleased? Are you pleased with what I am, where I am and what I'm doing?" Often times we're so busy looking around us that we may fail to pause to look within us. There are times when The Lord sees fit to draw us away from the crowd, the noise, the routine and the schedules, to set aside solitary time with Him. It's a time of awakening, refreshing and correction. He loves us enough to stop us in the middle of the routine and our so called agenda to show us what we really look like not to the world but to Him. It's a time when He inspects our garments ensuring that they have not become marred with works as opposed to spotless with worship!*

# THOUGHTS TO PONDER

*Wrong thinking got us where we are! The misunderstanding or mismanagement of our God given authority has caused us to conduct our affairs either illegally or ignorantly!*

*Wrong thinking has misaligned us! The plan of the enemy is to keep us focused on the negatives and seeing ourselves as inferior victims, which we are not. We are spiritual beings living in a physical body which mobilizes us and gives us the legal right to operate in the earth realm! Our spirituality empowers us so that we can exercise the dominion that God has given us. The mind is one of the most relevant powerhouses given to us by Our Father that is why the enemy attacks our minds. If you can destroy, contaminate ,manipulate or frustrate the mind of an individual you can ultimately control or immobilize that individual! This corrupts our understanding of who we are and what we were created to be or born to do, consequently purporting ones purpose.*

*Have you ever really wondered who you really are and what it is that you were born to do?*

*Have you ever looked into your own eyes and knew that there was more than just your pupil and retina but instead the essence of who you really are waiting for the moment when you would reach out and connect with her inviting her to live in the world that you know in exchange to live in the world that she knows?*

*I believe that our soul, our true self longs for the day when we connect so that we can experience the abundant life that lies awaiting for us.*

*It's that connection that fortifies our spiritual conviction and unleashes the power that God has ordained to be at work in us and through us! This power recharges us and energizes us giving us the zeal to introduce others to this liberty and vitality. It is unselfish and desires not to be used to take advantage of others that are misaligned!*

*When you know who you are you don't have to try to force yourself into someone else's world or Clique because you realize you have a place that God has ordained just for you and within that place is your designated role. It's a Role that is marshalled by God alone because you were assigned by Him.*

*I now understand demonic possession. It's the hijacking of the body, spirit and mind of an individual to utilize their legal right to have dominion!*

*SEE Ecclesiastes 9:11*

*SEE Genesis 1:27*

# Pursue your Passion

*When God tells us to pursue, it's his way of resting his seal of approval on the situation. The command is a declaration and assurance of victory causing failure to become the impossibility. When God says pursue, everything and everyone that we need is already in place to birth forth success beyond our greatest imagination! When God says pursue it's the command to go with heaven heralding victory! There's no need to ponder or wonder! It's the greatest most effective and affluent validation one could ever receive .when the almighty says pursue,it means you've been granted the official sanction .his sanction is His official approval for your action*

*When God says pursue a thing it's your authorization to move forward, matters not whether faith or friends waver. Meet me here at the place of your sanction and I will go. I'll dance to the song that you play as long as you're my partner. It doesn't matter if the song is unfamiliar to me. I know that you believe in what you have placed in me and I have both heaven and earth's support.*

*Access granted!!*

*It means I'm equipped with everything that I need for this next big move. I'm both certified and qualified!*

*Yielded, certified, qualified, called and chosen!*

**Pursue your passion!**

# THERE IS A CAUSE, OBEDIENCE IS A MUST!

*There were days when I felt like giving up and giving in. Hope didn't seem like an option that was available to me. I could literally hear words "why do you keep trying? Accept the defeat; it will make things less complicated; stop thinking, hoping, praying and expecting it to get better. You'd save yourself the frustration." The truth is at times I was convinced that these words were the reality of what is for me. My natural senses added the words "you can only be disappointed when you have expectations!"*

*Changing those thoughts were like trying to swim against a raging current. The harder you attempt to go against the current the further away hope appeared. Meanwhile weariness set in like rigor mortis.*

*How could someone with so much hope and potential be so engulfed in so much chaos?*

*Can you imagine feeling like there is no mortal being that you can share this experience with?*

*Generations are held in captivity by your disobedience and rejection of God! Likewise your obedience to the true and living God breaks down ancient barriers and strongholds giving way to deliverance breakthrough and victory! There is power at work in your yes Lord! Your bloodline is transfused by the soul cleansing blood of Jesus Christ who completes the work of redemption! Your right standing breaks the enemy's fetters from the lives of many! Do not become weary in well doing! Become slaves of righteousness so that you and others may be set free! Your righteous seed is germinating; it will produce fruit after its kind!*

# THE AFFLICTED SOULS.

*Enslavement, poverty and sickness are all diseases of the Adamic nature! We honour the things that God opposes which results in our being yoked by an umbilical cord which is attached to our past generations by way of our biological parents. Many are therefore bound by the spirit of rejection, bitterness, abandonment, ridicule, poverty, deceit and all the other weights and sins that enslaved our parents. Unless Jesus the Christ performs spiritual surgery and sever these ties we can never be free from them. As beautiful, strong and successful as we appear to be, when we look through the eyes of the spirit we see shackles and chains and with our spiritual ears we hear the LOUD deafening noise they make and the screams of the tormented souls that are bound by them. Freedom only comes through the acceptance of Jesus Christ as Lord and Saviour who has earned us the right to be liberated souls.*

# THE WELL OF FAITH

*Sometimes the well of your faith will begin to run dry. It's at those times you must dig deeper and plunge relentlessly into the ever springing well of God's word and replenish the well of your faith. Even as the brook Cherith sustained the Prophet Elijah so will God's word sustain us in the parched places of life. Unlike The Cherith, this great brook never runs dry. Sometimes even in the midst of great crowds we can experience loneliness especially when what we perceive to be our support system stands still in quietness to the point where it appears absent. Just like the 7000 prophets in Elijah's story, people are paralysed by fear or the vicissitudes of life. There are times when God chooses to lead us one step at a time which to the natural senses could be frightening because it is in our nature to want to know! To operate by logic has been classified as wisdom. In times of loneliness dependence on God becomes critical. I never imagined that loneliness was a type of training. It's training in yielding, training in surrender, training for service, training for standing and training in one's ability to trust. It is also one of the places where faith is solidified.*

*Although Cherith was a place of provision it has also proven to be the place of testing. Cherith is derived from the ancient Hebrew root meaning to cut away, to cut up or off. This denotes stripping, tearing and separation. Separation has its discomforts but it yields a far more exceeding weight of glory.*

# SUBTLE DISTRACTIONS

*The adversary has subtly found so many ways to distract us. If I read my bible as much as I did my Facebook updates or communed with the Father as often as I have my WhatsApp contacts I'd look more like Him and less like the world. I believe Father has so much to say to you and I but some doors has to be shut. Our gates (eyes, ears, heart, mind and spirit) need to be spiritually sanitized.*

*Awaken the Giant within!*

# GOD IN MAN, MADE MANIFEST

*It's amazing how we try to harden our hearts and shut our bowels of mercy yet love keeps finding a way to flow in and out.*

# ZION! QUICK MARCH! ~ INTERCESSION MUST BEGIN!!!

### Prayer

*Father, in the name of Jesus, enable us to be skilful intercessors as we take our rightful position within your kingdom, our homes and spheres of influence! Sharpen us as your instruments and allow us to be vigilant concerning the devices of the adversary! Help us not to get distracted, displaced or detoured by the strategies of the adversary! Give us the grace and fortitude we need to manoeuvre in life through prayer, praise worship and warfare! Father, stand guard over the investment that you have made in us! We cancel every plot, plan and scheme of the enemy to cause us to suffer spiritual or physical miscarriages in the name of Jesus!*

*God cause us to hear and to heed your voice! Be our compass and our guide! Adorn us with the fruit of your Holy Spirit. Stir up godly passion within us and penetrate the walls of any stronghold in our lives! Break down the walls of partition that seek to keep us from spending intimate time with you. Father, expose the lies that we may have accepted as truth! Break down any satanic altars we may have erected in our hearts or homes knowing or unknowingly! Remove resentment, pride, anger, un-forgiveness, hurt, rejection, bitterness, fear, rebelliousness, offense and stubbornness far from us that we may be vessels of honour fit for your use. Remove the scales from our eyes that we may see from your perspective! Open our ears to hear! Make our hearts fertile grounds for your word! Father, reveal yourself to us and through us for our good and your glory! Saturate our hearts and homes with your sweet Holy Spirit! Spiritually sanitize us and guard the gates of our lives from every form of corruption. Anoint us afresh for the assignments you have given us in Jesus' mighty name!*

*Amen!*

# HURT AND OFFENSE HAS ALWAYS BEEN THE ADVERSARY'S WEAPONS!

*You may not be able to change the entire world or assist everyone in need but you've been placed in the position to POSITIVELY INFLUENCE YOUR SPHERE WITH THE MESSAGE, AUTHORITY AND POWER OF THE GOSPEL! The spirit of offense is dangerous at the gate! It hampers prayers and vigilance!*

# AUDIENCE OF ONE! PRAYER

Sometimes it is in simplicity that we are most effective! Seek to please an audience of one (GOD). Go back to his first instructions, the initial conversation. It's not about showing how much we know. It's about hearing the father's heart and getting his attention.

# WORDS OF CONSOLATION

If I allow the enemy to squeeze you he will only draw out the investments I've made in you!

# PRAYER

Father, I pray that the spirit of intercession would break out over this nation! I pray that intercessors would come out of slumber and take their rightful place upon the walls of the city! I pray that we would no longer dwell at ease in Zion but that we would stand between the earth and heaven and travail on behalf of our nation and its people, understanding that in doing so we cover all grounds! Hedge us in by your grace and mercy! Cause our spirits to comply with the urgency of the call! Cause our motives and agenda to be pleasing to you. Enable us to walk by faith and assume our rightful positions as priests, gatekeepers and watchmen! Forgive us for leaving our positions unmanned giving the enemy leeway! We cover our waters, our borders and airspace in the blood of Jesus! We seal our islands and cays in the blood of Jesus! We cover our armed forces and those that protect our waters and borders and seal them in the blood of Jesus! We cover our schools, churches, homes, vehicles and possessions that you have given to us under the blood of Jesus! We loose salvation, revival, conviction, correction, healing, restoration and *deliverance in the name of Jesus! We bind every spirit and system that opposes your precepts, your word and your will for this country and its people! Cause the fire of the Holy Spirit to rain and reign in this nation! Replace the hearts of stone with hearts of flesh! We thank you for redemption by the power of the crucifixion and resurrection of our Saviour and Lord Jesus Christ! Cause a great teruah to break out over our nation so that every spiritual wall of Jericho will come down and every idol and satanic altar be broken in pieces in Jesus' name for our good and your glory. Amen!*

**Many are out of position because they have miscalculated God's instruction!**

# OBSTACLES

*Use your obstacles like a trapezium! Scale new heights by allowing the depths to propel you beyond your so called limitations.*

### Gentle Giant~ Pastor Beatrice Knowles

*She taught me what I would call gentle warfare ~ meekness and humility that can break the back of the enemy consequently dismantling his strongholds.*

*She reminds me so much of Jesus who was and is both the Lion and the Lamb! Though her speech is mild in temperament it's weighty in conviction. Truly she influences with the message, authority and power of the gospel of Jesus Christ. She inspires me to say yes to the Lord constantly.*

# IT'S NOT TOO LATE! (JUN.11.15)

*It's not too late to start doing what it is you really want or were born to do! Busyness is sometimes a distraction. When I ask something of you do it with what you have. Do not say why it cannot be done!*

**I am your provision, submit!**

**When I meet with God muddy water becomes crystal clear!**

# LOOKING OUT FOR WHAT GOD SAID ~ THE WAIT OF THE APPOINTED TIME

*There were days when I felt like Elijah's servant looking out multiple times for the rain of God's promises. I heard the voice of The Father telling me what is and what is to come to satisfy the voice of my supplications that were before Him; some I considered immediate needs others I classified as my heart's desire. Many days the facts steered me in the face and the only thing I could hold on to was the truth of Gods faithfulness to His word and character. With tears in my eyes I'd have to convince me that what He said, He would do. If He spoke a word, it shall and will come to pass. Though the visions tarry I wait even if it meant crying as I did.*

*And the LORD answered me, and said, Write the vision, and make it plain upon tables, that he may run that readeth it.*

*3 For the vision is yet for an appointed time, but at the end it shall speak, and not lie: though it tarry, wait for it; because it will surely come, it will not tarry. (Habakkuk 2:2KJV)*

# THE DAMASCUS ROAD EXPERIENCE

*Every one of us will one day have a Damascus Road Experience. For me it was rejection. I found myself being rejected by people that I loved; persons I have connected myself to be it spiritually or emotionally. I was rejected by people that I loved. Rejection was the place where I found God and where I believe that He found me. It wasn't that He was at any time absent, but it was the place where I became intentional about my relationship with Him. There were many days when it was just God and me which was actually the majority but in my finite wisdom I was in the minority.*

*What is a Damascus Road experience one might ask? In my opinion Damascus is a place of transformation, brokenness, inspiration, humility and intimacy. It is a place of many questions and woe to which God alone has the answers and solutions.*

*Sometimes it is the immeasurable grace and love of God that leads our Prodigals through the Damascus Road experience so that they too may have that personal encounter with Him. In our finite wisdom and because of our "storge or familial love" we pray that they never go that way. Damascus though a place of intimacy takes on the form of isolation. I was in prayer for a loved one who was in the midst of a dark situation and the Holy Spirit whispered "Damascus is necessary! "Though the issue itself bore a weight the words of the Holy Spirit brought peace, comfort and the assurance that ALL WAS WELL.*

# TRANSITION

*Transition is an amazing vehicle. The ride can sometimes be so vigorous that you could actually lose equilibrium. God's divine purpose has been* the seatbelt that has kept me safe through some of the most tumultuous rides. God kept me! There were days when my personal GPS just didn't seem to function. I felt as though I had no sense of direction. God in His infinite wisdom altered my circumstances, my spiritual climate and my emotional location to accommodate His divine will, allowing all things to work together for my good. He loved, called and chastised me. A **call** is never seen, it's heard.

## SHE HAS ALWAYS BELIEVED IN ME.

I'm so grateful that sometimes repetition is necessary to get IT right. Often times it's during the tedious task of doing things over and repeatedly that important information surfaces. God has placed some Gems in my life who at one point or the other has served in the capacity of midwives in my many attempts to Birth my precious seeds. A few of them are the late Sylvia Davis, the late Eulease Dames, Gaynell Robinson, Dorothy Grant, Eva Hilton, Maud Beverley Culmer, Maria Hamilton, Mabelline Hemmings, Shantell Sturrup Cassius, Sandra Johnson, Pastor Helen Mcphee, Prophetess Joan Laing, Maude Beverly, Minister Claudine Smith and of course Pastor Cleopatra Williams, thank you for ALWAYS believing in me. God has allowed me to be nurtured, mothered and supported by so many strong yet graceful women of God. Some I call friends/ sisters, you know who you are. I love you.

*I use to wish that I could have done it all over but that was before I came to the realization that every heart ache, heart break, disappointment, rejection, bad decision, dysfunctional relationship, misunderstanding, apparent missed opportunity, isolation, separation, failure, apparent mistake has strategically positioned me into the perfect will of God. They have validated my calling and fashioned me into God's chosen vessel of honor. I was rejected to be chosen, last to be first, beneath to be exalted above, surrounded by enemies so that my table could be spread, led to the valley to show others the way to God's holy mountain. I was allowed to be engaged in constant warfare to be made more than a conqueror through the greater one who dwells within me .I was hidden in the secret place so that under His shadow I'd learn to abide .He's forever faithful. I am grateful to my spiritual sisters Ashley Outten, Yvonne Stubbs, Jackie Turner and Italia Duncanson; they literally carried me in prayer many days disregarding what I considered my failures. They continued to call me by the name God had given me and not the name I may have in weakness acted out.*

# "DADDY'S GIRL

Without this paragraph this message of inspiration would be incomplete. Although I struggled with the lesson my earthly Father taught me what it meant to truly be content. He is the epitome of a content soul. My father sees the good in everything and anything. I cannot recall a negative remark ever coming from his lips regarding the issues of life despite his love for causing spontaneous laughter. Up to this point in time of my life I can only remember us having two struggles in our relationship. Those we worked out quickly. One of my fondest memories was the time we actually cried together. It remains our personal joke though that day the circumstances was not funny at all but like I said my dad will find the good in it. He has encouraged me at some of the lowest times in my life without even knowing it. We always refer to mothers when we speak of maternal instincts. This maternal instinct is thought to be responsible for certain types of behavior. My dad always seems to call with the right words when my spirit is crushed. He always seems to respond to my issues without any indication on my part that there is a problem. *(A word fitly spoken is like apples of gold in pictures of silver. Proverbs 25:11-13). Truth be told I'll always be a daddy's girl.*

# THE STRUGGLE OF BEING PECULIAR

Many years I struggled with the desire to be considered ordinary denying the truth that has called and predestined me to be peculiar. I fought against purpose and my destiny often times miscalculating it as opposition that came from others. The truth is, they were reflecting like the image in a mirror that which was being projected from within me. The greatest battles that we will ever face are the internal ones that rage like opposing currents within the same body of water which violently churns swallowing anything and everything in its path that is vulnerable.

To be peculiar is the complete opposite of being ordinary. In fact it is to be the extraordinary which is driven by none other than the power greater than everything that is created. It is to be set apart, unfamiliar, unpredictable, strange, unique and exclusive. It never fits into what is considered to be the "norm" or average. It never blends in but instead it stands out. It is not defined by anything or anyone other than He who is the creator of its kind. It cannot be contained or restricted by another created thing without causing turbulence of some kind. It may function but outside of its rightful place it creates raging currents that drives it to unleash, opposing what is accepted as ordinary.

Don't be afraid to embrace the fact that the frame from which you were designed was exclusively formed with you alone in mind.

# MOTION SICKNESS

Motion sickness is those emotions that you experience when following your dreams. They often lead you away from the nest of familiarity that you always knew as home. It's the tearing away that causes discomforts because moving towards your destiny requires you to adjust your sails to charter new territories. It's a discomfort that you feel when you are at your crossroad and you're closer to your destiny than you've ever been.

# THE GREATEST PERSUASION

Why do you rely on someone else's behavior towards you to authenticate my call on your life? Why are you more persuaded by their actions or inactions rather than my response? Have I not proven to you that you are mine, yet still you question that which I have ordained and that which I have spoken concerning you.

# THE CONCLUSION OF THE MATTER

I am releasing this work understanding that to some it may be far from perfect based on standards that have been set by mortals like me. I am certain that according to the English professors there are some things that perhaps could have been written differently. I made an attempt to make sure this was perfect and in the midst of the attempt I realized that "the message" is perfect and that's what really matters. Additionally, perfection comes with practice, just begin! You see, sometimes we have got to be prepared to start right where we are understanding that God may not call to be used those that others consider equipped or perfect but often times He chooses to equip those that He has called. Perfection may be ordained to come as progress is made. God has a reputation for using those that are considered "broken vessels." I struggled with this truth even though my life is proof of it. I don't know who you are, what you may have done, what you have been told by others or perhaps what you may have told yourself but God wants you to know this, "you are not beyond repair and yes you can be used, you just need to be yielded and available." Whatever He has given you to do, JUST DO IT! When you obey God, He breathes on your seed of obedience and causes it to produce life. With Him YOU ARE GOOD ENOUGH TO BE USED!

Printed in the United States
By Bookmasters